BEAVER SCAMPERS THROUGH YELLOWSTONE

Follow Along As He Explores the Park

Written by Jaxine Harris
Illustrated by Joan Coleman

THIS BOOK BELONGS TO:

_____

ABOUT THE AUTHOR

Jaxine Harris is from historic Oregon City, Oregon, known for being the end of the Oregon Trail. She grew up on a small family farm and now resides in Lake Oswego, Oregon.

Family vacations were spent camping and visiting national parks. She fell in love with the grand lodges, watching wildlife, and hiking the many trails.

After college, wanderlust took her to Europe where she traveled and worked in Switzerland and Germany.

Teaching was a passion and she taught for 28 years. After retirement, wanderlust struck again, taking her to Yellowstone. She worked ten summer seasons in the historic lodges, watched wildlife, and hiked the many trails.

Contact Jaxine at jaxine.beaver@gmail.com.

ABOUT THE ILLUSTRATOR

Joan Coleman is a professional artist and book illustrator. She and her husband, Andrew, own and operate Ink Wonderland, an illustration and design company that provides graphic design, illustration, and apparel design services for clients all across the USA. To learn more about Ink Wonderland please visit www.inkwonderland.com.

WHERE IS YELLOWSTONE NATIONAL PARK?

On the United States map, find Yellowstone and color it.
Find the state you live in, and color it.
How far away do you live from the park?

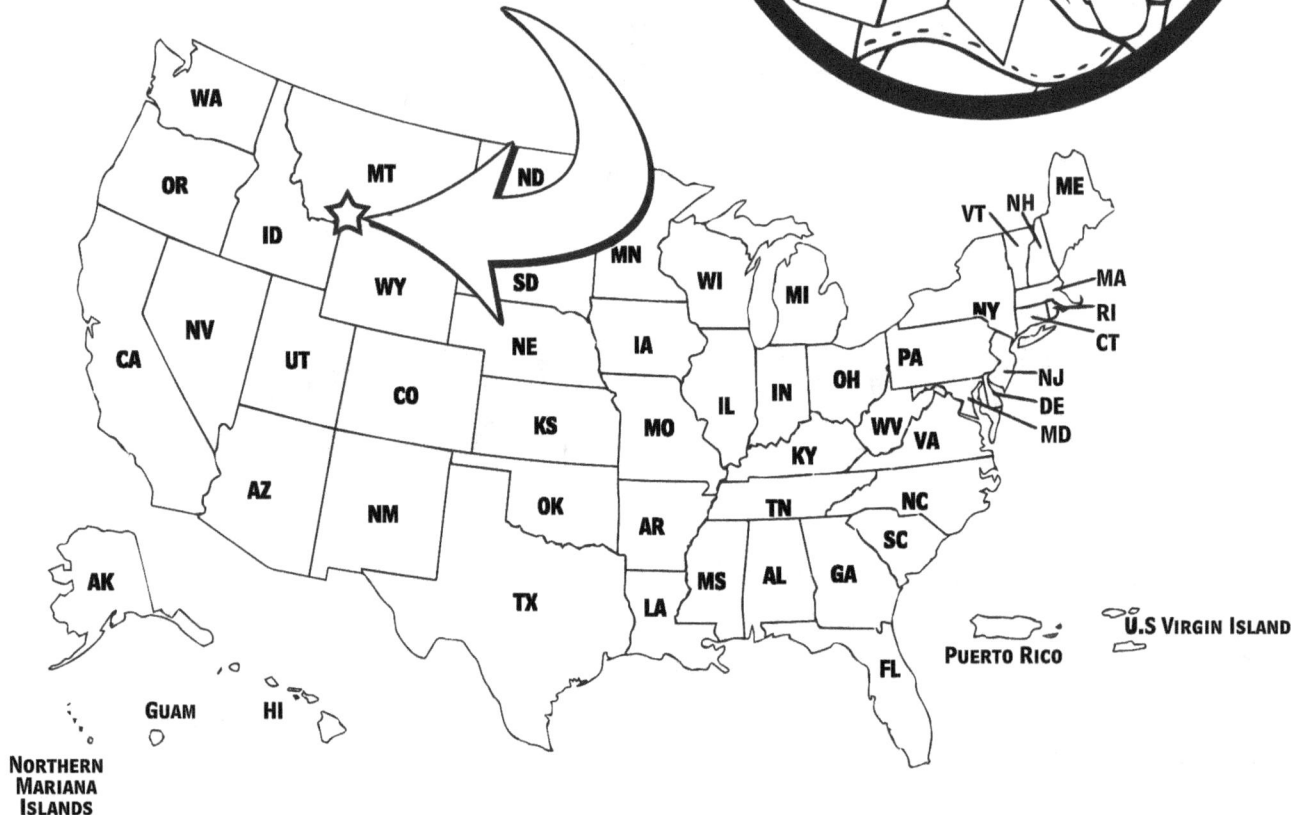

**96% of Yellowstone Park is in Wyoming, known as the Cowboy State.
The park boundaries spill into Montana (3%) and Idaho (1%).**

MAP OF YELLOWSTONE NATIONAL PARK

Follow Beaver on the map, as he scampers through the park.
The Yellowstone grand loop road circles around like the number 8.

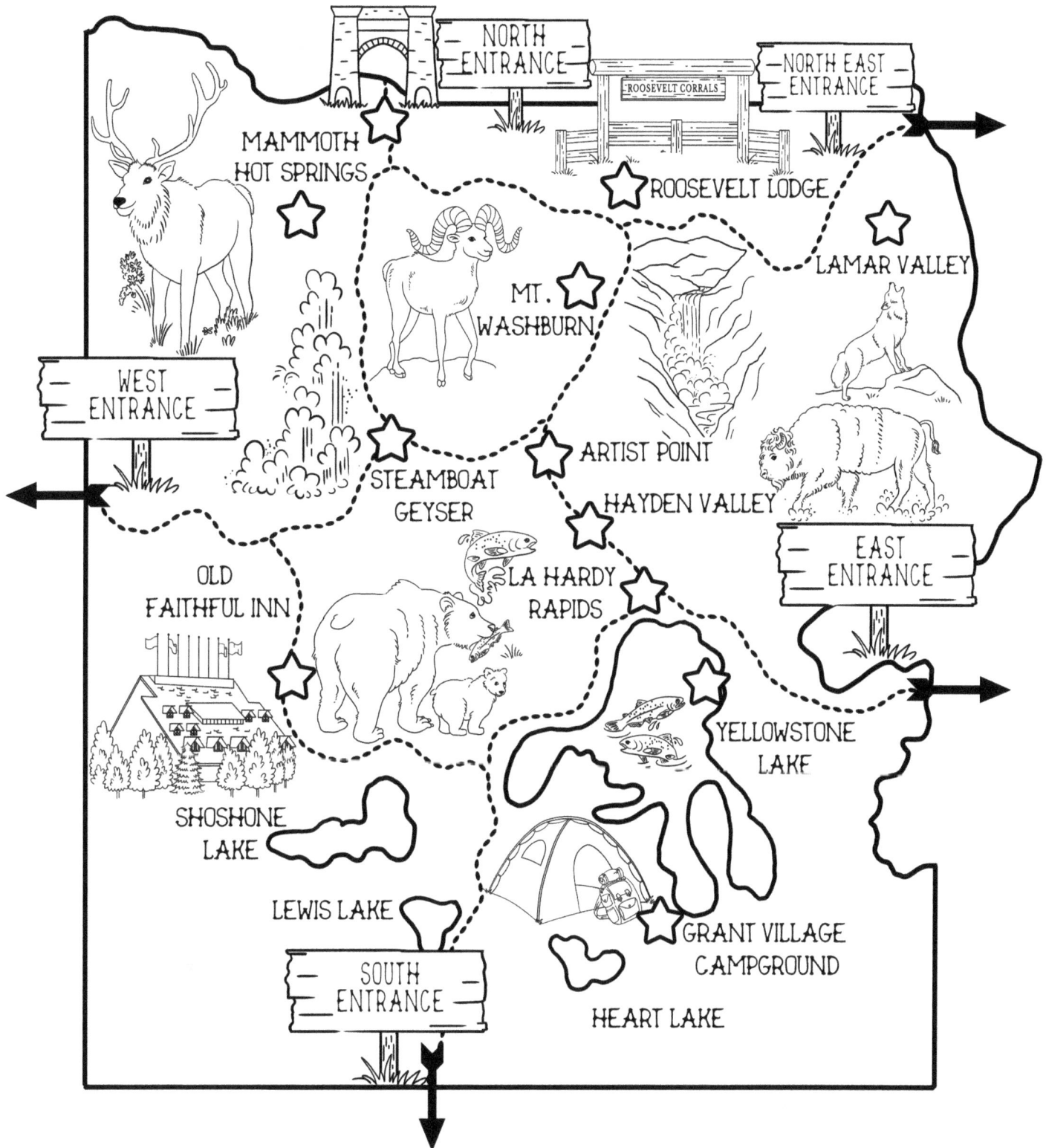

NORTH ENTRANCE

NORTH EAST ENTRANCE

ROOSEVELT CORRALS

MAMMOTH HOT SPRINGS

ROOSEVELT LODGE

LAMAR VALLEY

MT. WASHBURN

WEST ENTRANCE

STEAMBOAT GEYSER

ARTIST POINT

HAYDEN VALLEY

EAST ENTRANCE

OLD FAITHFUL INN

LA HARDY RAPIDS

YELLOWSTONE LAKE

SHOSHONE LAKE

LEWIS LAKE

GRANT VILLAGE CAMPGROUND

SOUTH ENTRANCE

HEART LAKE

THINGS TO DO, SEE, AND LEARN IN YELLOWSTONE NATIONAL PARK

Cross activities off as you complete them

PHOTOGRAPHY

HIKING

RANGER TALKS

VISIT THE VISITOR CENTERS

BUY A BOOK AND READ ABOUT YELLOWSTONE

GEYSER GAZING

HORSEBACK TRAIL RIDES

STAGECOACH RIDES

ROOSEVELT CHUCKWAGON COOKOUTS

BIKE RIDING – rent or ride your own, follow the rules

GET YOUR JR. RANGER BADGE

BUS TOURS

YELLOWSTONE LAKE CRUISES

FISHING

DOUBLE DECKER ICE CREAM CONES ARE GREAT ON HOT DAYS

EAT SOME NEW FOODS – try a bison burger, elk sausage, huckleberry ice cream, candy, and pancakes

GAZE AT THE NIGHT SKY –Pick out the milky way and the big dipper

ATTEND THE EVENING CAMPFIRE RANGER TALKS

WATCH FOR DOUBLE RAINBOWS – If the weather is just right

ANIMAL WATCHING – FROM A DISTANCE

MEET BEAVER!

Beaver is a fun-loving, friendly
fellow who loves adventure.
He is going on an exciting
sightseeing trip to find wildlife,
thermal features, waterfalls, lakes,
canyons, and meadows. His camera is
ready, as he explores our nation's
first national park – Yellowstone.

BEAVER HAS MANY SKILLS
He can read maps
Pitch tents
Build campfires
Make yummy s'mores
And gnaw sticks faster than lightning,
for roasting marshmallows

He also has a QUIRKY habit – Beaver FLAPS his tail –
A LOT, when excited!

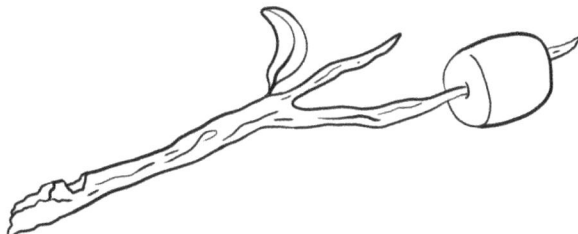

Beaver arrives in Yellowstone – at last,
Knowing this adventure will be a blast.

Beaver sees the famous arch with words etched in stone
And snaps lots of pictures using his brand new phone.

He follows directions on a huge park map.
Excited, off he goes, FLAPPITY – FLAP – FLAP!

MAMMOTH
HOT SPRINGS
VILLAGE

Travertine Terraces glisten snowy white.
Beaver is amazed; it's an awesome sight.

A bull elk is grazing on the Mammoth lawn.
He could be there all evening, into early dawn.

Where to next? Beaver follows the map.
Off he goes, FLAPPITY – FLAP – FLAP!

The Roosevelt area is cowboy land.
It's rustic and wild for any cowhand.

Beaver straddles a horse and rides a trail,
Bouncing along, up and down on his tail.

Where to next? Beaver follows the map.
Off he goes, FLAPPITY – FLAP – FLAP!

Lamar Valley is where wolves howl.
Beaver wonders if they're on the prowl.
Where wolves are, there might be a raven.
There are many, all misbehavin'.

Where to next? Beaver follows the map.
Off he goes, FLAPPITY – FLAP – FLAP!

LAMAR VALLEY

MT WASHBURN
ELEV. 10,243 FT
ELEV. 3,122 M

Beaver climbs Mt. Washburn to the fire lookout.
"10,000 feet – I made it," he gives a BIG shout!
Beaver looks around, and doesn't hear a peep.
But he looks again, and sees a big horn sheep.

Where to next? Beaver follows the map.
Off he goes, FLAPPITY – FLAP – FLAP!

THE LOWER FALLS
GRAND CANYON OF
YELLOWSTONE

The Grand Canyon of Yellowstone is an awesome sight.
Beaver hikes the rim and sees an osprey taking flight.

He hikes to Artist Point and is stunned by the view.
The lower falls roar loudly and spray drops of dew.

Where to next? Beaver follows the map.
Off he goes, FLAPPITY – FLAP – FLAP!

Hayden Valley is a huge, open space.
Lots of waterfowl swim at this place.
Watch for pelicans with funny bills.
Trumpeter swans preening will give you thrills.

HAYDEN VALLEY

Friendly Fox says, "How do you do!"
Beaver squeaks, "Just fine, how are you?"
"Let's be friends," Fox grins with glee.
"We'll be a team, you and me!"

A herd of bison thunder past,
Hundreds crossing the road – AT LAST!
Beaver and Fox scramble out of the way.
This is an ANIMAL JAM, rangers say.

Where to next? The two new friends follow the map.
Off they go, FLAPPITY – FLAP – FLAP!

Beaver hears rapids making a roar.
The cutthroats are jumping, one – two – three – four!

Where to next? The two friends follow the map.
Off they go, FLAPPITY – FLAP – FLAP!

-LA HARDY RAPIDS-
YELLOWSTONE RIVER

Beaver goes fishing and takes a ride – – –
On Yellowstone lake, so deep and wide.
Fox goes, too, and catches a trout.
"YIPPY – A BIG ONE!" he gives a LOUD shout.

"LOOK," yells Fox, "way over there – – –
I see a huge brown grizzly bear!"
It's lunchtime for mom and little cub.
Cutthroat trout makes yummy grub.

Where to next? The two friends follow the map.
Off they go, FLAPPITY – FLAP – FLAP!

Old Faithful is erupting, look how high it goes!
Beaver feels it rumbling, clear through his toes.

Thrilled, Beaver's tail goes FLAPPITY – FLAP – FLAP!

OLD FAITHFUL
GEYSER

Beaver whispers, "MY – OH – MY!"
He looks up at flags waving high.
The Old Faithful Inn is rustic and grand,
With huge logs and beams, all made by hand.
Fox looks at Beaver with a sly grin,
Thinking wouldn't it be fun if they could sneak in.

Squeezing through a hole that Fox once dug,
They race across a BIG – BLACK – BEAR – RUG!
Up the rafters they Q-U-I-C-K-L-Y scurry!
Down the rafters they R-E-A-L-L-Y hurry!
WHEW! Back outside and on their way,
They've had a lot of fun this day.

They sniff something funny – and follow their nose.
Maybe it's a MUDPOT, do you suppose?

The smell of rotten eggs fills the air.
Thermal features are everywhere.
PLOP – PLOP – BUBBLE – BLOT - - -
Are the sounds of a gooey mudpot.
Lots of hissing steam from a great big hole,
But no water – it's called a fumarole.

STEAMBOAT
GEYSER

DRAGON'S MOUTH
AT MUD VOLCANO
AREA

MUDPOT

COLOR BY NUMBER: 1 blue, 2 green, 3 yellow, 4 orange, 5 brown

Fox and Beaver scoot along the boardwalks,
Listening to rangers give special talks - - -
About why hot water comes from the ground,
Creating amazing colors all around.

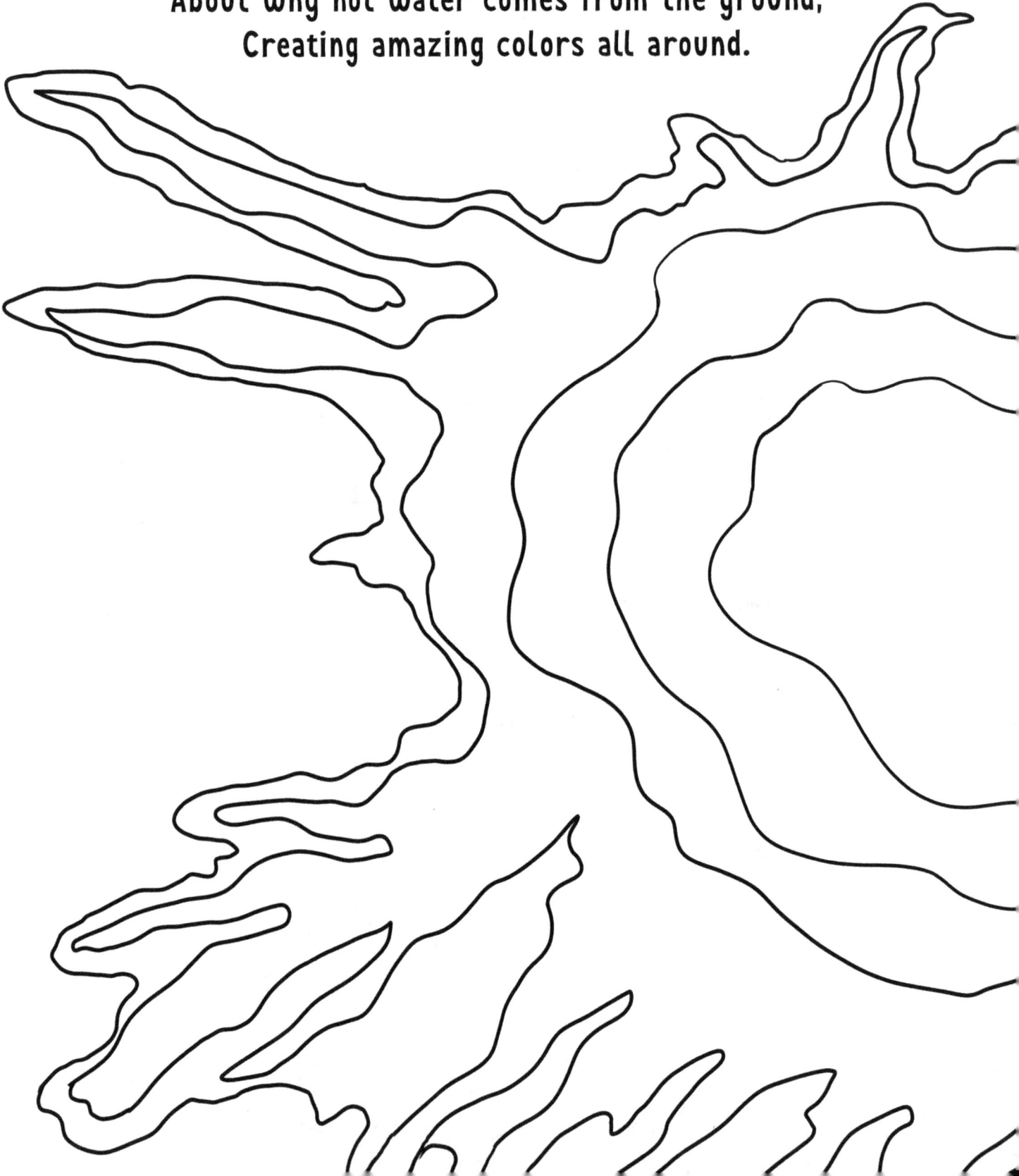

Where to next? Excited, the two friends follow the map.
Off they go, FLAPPITY – FLAP – FLAP!

GRAND PRISMATIC
HOTSPRING

1 2 3 4 5

The visitor centers are fun places to go,
Filled with books, games, and good things to know.
Each center is different; they all have a theme.
Visit them all, and you'll know what I mean.

OLD FAITHFUL
VISITOR CENTER

JUNIOR
RANGER
YELLOWSTONE

Friendly to tourists are the park rangers,
Informing them of Yellowstone dangers.
They tell stories and lead hikes,
But once in awhile, they'll yell Y-I-K-E-S!
Obey the rules, and you won't get hurt - - -
Signs are everywhere, so be on A-L-E-R-T!

Where to next? SLEEPY, the two friends follow the map.
Off they go, FLAPPITY – FLAP – FLAP!

DO NOT FEED WILDLIFE

NEVER HIKE ALONE

Have fun! Be safe!

STAY ON THE BOARDWALK IN THERMAL AREAS

Be Alert!

STOP, LOOK and LISTEN!

DANGER DO NOT APPROACH WILDLIFE

WHEN CAMPING USE BEAR BOXES AND PUT OUT THE CAMPFIRE

RANGER TALK-TONIGHT
TOPIC-WOLVES

Beaver is tired; he's had a long day.
He looks for a campground where he can stay.
He asks friend Fox to spend the night.
They pitch a tent in a quiet campsite.

The campfire crackles as the flames lick high.
"Look," whispers Beaver, "at that Yellowstone sky!"
Many forest friends have gathered and stayed,
Sharing the s'mores that Beaver made.

GRAHAM
CRACKERS

CAMPGROUND
GRANT VILLAGE

A new friend, Coyote, joins the group
And does some tricks to entertain the troop.
Fox is happy curled up in his tail,
Beaver's dreaming the good life – all is well.

Scampering through Yellowstone has come to an end.
Beaver had a blast and made new friends.
He learned a lot and saw many things.
He'll remember the thrill that adventure brings.

NATIONAL PARK SERVICE

Safe journeys my friend!

Leaving

YELLOWSTONE NATIONAL PARK

YELLOWSTONE NATIONAL PARK

WHAT DID BEAVER SEE?

Do you remember what Beaver saw and experienced?
Answer the questions and fill in the squares

Across

2 What animal did Beaver see at the Travertine Terraces?

5 What geyser is the largest in the world?

7 What flies high on top of the Old Faithful Inn?

10 What is the name of the valley where Beaver saw wolves and ravens?

11 Do visitor centers each have their own theme? Yes or No

12 What kind of bear was having cutthroat trout for lunch?

13 What lookout is on top of Mt. Washburn?

14 On what lake did Beaver and Fox go fishing?

15 What kind of sheep does Beaver see on Mt. Washburn?

Down

1 When Beaver gets excited, what does his tail do?

2 The Yellowstone grand loop road circles around like what number?

3 Geysers, mud pots, fumaroles, and hot springs are called _____ features.

4 What is the name of the area where Beaver rode a horse?

6 Dragon's Mouth is in a thermal area called _____ Volcano.

8 The famous Roosevelt Arch is in what town in Montana?

9 What is the name of the valley where Beaver met Fox?

FIND THE BEAVER POND

Beaver followed one of the marked trails while he scampered through Yellowstone. To his surprise, he found a BEAVER POND.
See if you can find the pond. But, AVOID the bear.
What do you think is in and around beaver ponds? Hint – see below!

START

FINISH

THE BEAVER POND AND DAM

Beavers gnaw down trees and build dams on rivers and lakes. Beaver dams are very strong. The dams create ponds, which help improve the Yellowstone ecosystem. How? When a pond is formed, more wildlife is attracted to it, creating a circle of life.

Frogs leap from rock to rock, and ribbit their favorite song.
Brook trout wiggle and make a ripple as they swim along.
Dragonflies snap and other insects buzz,
The blue heron struts through cottonwood fuzz.
Moose submerge under water and chomp on plants.
Osprey dive and fly, it's fun to watch them dance.

FUN FACTS ABOUT WILDLIFE

Trumpeter Swan
These swans are the largest waterfowl in North America. They are snowy-white, with black beaks. Yellowstone is only one of several places in the world where visitors can see them. Watch for them in slow-moving waters or lakes.

Moose
A funny looking animal with large paddle-like antlers and long legs. The antlers can weigh up to 80 lbs. Dangling under the throat is loose skin and hair called a dewlap or "bell." If you are lucky, you might see one in the Lamar Valley near Soda Butte Creek, and closer to the NE entrance.

Elk
There are lots and lots of elk In the park. The Shawnee tribe called the elk "wapiti," which means "white-rumped deer." Their antlers grow very high and are referred to as a "rack." When the old "rack" is shed, new growth begins and grows fast, 2/3 to 1 inch a day. In the fall, visitors can hear the males "bugle." Elk can be seen at Mammoth Hot Springs in September, all over the area.

Bighorn Sheep
A magnificent animal. They like high, rocky areas and are sure-footed for the habitat. Both male and females have horns, but eventually the male horns begin to curve. These horns can weigh 40 lbs. The males are called "rams." When fighting, they "ram" or butt their heads together. In the summers, visitors can see them on Mt. Washburn and Dunraven Pass.

Yellow-Bellied Marmot
They are one of the largest rodents in Yellowstone. They like open grassy areas near rocks. They make a "whistle" sound and have been called "whistle pigs." Look for them sunning themselves at Storm Point Overlook.

Raven
These birds are of the crow family. They are very big, very smart, and very naughty. They can get into your back pack, take your food, unzip items, and peck apart the seats of bikes. Be aware! The history of ravens and wolves as a "team" goes back to ancient times. They follow each other to dead animals for food. Ravens often follow the wolves on an elk hunt. Listen for their funny sounds.

The Gray Wolf
The wolves were introduced back into the park in 1995 and 1996. They came from Canada and were released in Lamar Valley. These wolves were named the Druid pack. The wolves improved the Yellowstone ecosystem.

Bison – Nickname Buffalo
Bison wander all through the park, but large herds can be seen in Lamar and Hayden Valleys. Native Americans used every part of the animal for survival: meat for food, hides for warmth, and the horns, hooves, and bones for tools. They used dung for fire fuel. Stay 25 yards away.

Bears – Two Kinds
Both grizzly bears and black bears have very sensitive noses and can smell things miles away. Grizzlies are larger than the black bears. If the hump behind the shoulder is higher than the rump, it's a grizzly. If the rump is higher than the shoulder hump, it's a black bear. Stay 100 yards away – that's a football field.

Fox
The little red fox weighs only 9-12 pounds. They hunt at night so seeing one is rare. They eat mice and other small rodents. Look for one in Lamar Valley and near the Canyon or Hayden Valley areas.

Pronghorn
The Pronghorn is NOT an antelope. They are very fast, running for several miles at 45 mph. The colors and markings make them very easy to identify. Both male and female have true horns. Only the male horns become pronged. They can be seen in the Lamar Valley.

Osprey
These are easily mistaken for bald eagles. They are smaller than the eagle and have a white belly. They build nests in high trees or on pinnacles close to water. There is a nest on a pinnacle in the Grand Canyon of Yellowstone.

YELLOWSTONE ANIMAL WORD FIND

Look for words — across, down, backwards, and diagonally

Beaver
Grizzly bear
Big horn sheep
Marmot
Bison
Moose
Black bear

Pronghorn
Chipmunk
River otter
Elk
Squirrel
Fox
Wolf

B I G H O R N S H E E P
E S O O M N L J J B R M
G R I Z Z L Y B E A R B
N E Y K X M W K D W L D
R T S O N O A G L A B D
O T F Q L U D R C E R R
H O N F U R M K M E Y R
G R O T J I B P V O V T
N E S V R E R A I R T P
O V I P A Q E R B H X K
R I B R M B T T E G C Y
P R G B M G N M W L B M

MATCHING
WRITE THE CORRECT ANSWERS BY THE QUESTIONS

What animal is also called a whistle pig? _____   Wolf

What is the nickname for the trees that are
white on the lower portion of the trunk? _____   Osprey

What is a Native American name for elk? _____   Trumpeter Swan

Native Americans called moose what name? _____   Yellow-bellied marmot

The word "buffalo" is a nickname for what animal?_____   Grand Prismatic

What famous geyser erupts every 90 minutes,
give or take 10 minutes? _____   Black

What geyser is the tallest in the world?_____   Rotten eggs

Sulfuric acid, released from some thermal
features, smells like what? _____   Steamboat

If the RUMP is higher than the HUMP behind the
shoulder, it is what kind of bear? _____   Twig eater

If the HUMP behind the shoulder is higher than the
RUMP, it is what kind of bear? _____   Bison

What waterfowl is the largest in North America?
It is found in only several places in the world.
Yellowstone is one of those places. _____   Old Faithful

What animal, released into the park in 1995
and 1996, helps improve the Yellowstone
ecosystem? _____   Grizzly

What hot spring is the largest in the park? _____   Wapiti

What bird is often mistaken for a bald eagle?
Visitors can see its nest on a pinnacle in the
Grand Canyon of Yellowstone. _____   Bobby sock

FUN FACTS ABOUT YELLOWSTONE

Size – 3,472 square miles larger than the states of Rhode Island and Delaware combined

Our Nation's 1st National Park

Yellowstone is our nation's 1st national park and the 1st national park in the world. Dedicated on March 1st 1872, by President Ulysses S. Grant.

Native flowers/plants – 1000 +

Waterfalls – 290

"For the Benefit and Enjoyment of the People"

The Roosevelt Arch is located in Gardiner, Montana. The words etched in stone on the arch symbolize why the park was established. Many visitors have pictures taken there.

Continental Divide From the south entrance to Old Faithful village, you cross it 3 times.

Tallest waterfall – The lower falls 308 feet in the Yellowstone River

Highest point – Eagle Peak at 11,358 feet

What is Yellowstone?

It is a live volcano. Many years ago, a huge eruption created a very large crater, called a caldera. It has filled in with dirt, rocks, trees, and water through the years. Because it is a live volcano, there are many thermal features that come from beneath the earth's surface.

Cutthroat trout – Are native to Yellowstone. If you catch one you need to release it.

Forests – 80% is lodgepole pine

Yellowstone Lake shoreline – 141 miles

Animals – 67 different kinds

Sheep Eaters

These were a small band of Shoshone Indians who made Yellowstone their home about 500 years ago. They hunted the bighorn sheep and used the animal for food, clothing, and tools. That is how they got their name. Other tribes came through Yellowstone as well but stayed only for the summer.

Rotten egg smell– from hydrogen sulfide gas very strong at Mud Volcano area

The Yellowstone River – 371 miles longest flowing undammed river in the the U.S.A.

Stagecoaches – Before cars, visitors traveled by stagecoach through the park.

The Fires of 1988

There were 51 fires total that summer. Nine of them were caused by people. Over 1/3rd of Yellowstone was burned. Many parts of the park have reforested themselves. There have been new fires since.

Birds – 285 different kinds

The Grand Canyon of Yellowstone – 20 to 22 miles long

Earthquakes – 2000 yearly on the average

Yellowstone's Name

In Montana the Yellowstone River had yellow sandstone cliffs. The Hidatsa Indians named the river "Rock Yellow River." They named it this because of the yellow cliffs. The Hidatsa word for "Rock Yellow River," was "Mi tse a-da-zi." The French trappers called it "Yellow Rock River" and the English speaking trappers called it the "Yellowstone River." So now, we have "Yellowstone."

Visitors yearly – over 4 million

Fishing –some of the best trout fishing in the world

MEMORIES OF YELLOWSTONE
Create Your Personal Diary
Write the Highlights of Your Adventure

WHAT ARE YOUR TWO MOST FUN EXPERIENCES IN YELLOWSTONE?

1.   2.

WHAT IS YOUR FAVORITE

Animal	Bird	Flower	Thermal Feature

ANSWER THE QUESTIONS BELOW

Did you receive a Jr. Ranger badge? Where did you receive it?

Did you gaze at the Yellowstone night sky? How many stars?

Name some thermal features you saw.

Did you eat a bison burger? Yum – Yum!

Did you attend a park ranger talk or go on a ranger hike?

What did you learn from the talk or on the hike?

Did you get into an animal jam? What animal or animals?

Did you stay in a hotel, a lodge, or camped?

SHOW AND TELL

When you go back to school, what will you tell your friends and family about your trip to Yellowstone? If your teacher asks the class to present "show and tell" about their summer vacation, what will you share with the class? Think about the things you wrote on these memory pages and include: where you stayed, pictures you took, souvenirs you collected, and any other things you saw, learned, and experienced. Write your thoughts below.

HAVE FUN!

_____

_____

_____

_____

_____

_____

_____

_____

_____

_____

_____

_____

Memories...

ANSWER KEY

MATCHING KEY

1) YELLOW-BELLIED MARMOT
2) BOBBY SOCK
3) WAPITI
4) TWIG EATER
5) BISON
6) OLD FAITHFUL
7) STEAMBOAT
8) ROTTEN EGGS
9) BLACK
10) GRIZZLY
11) TRUMPETER SWAN
12) WOLF
13) GRAND PRISMATIC
14) OSPREY

CROSSWORD PUZZLE KEY

WORD FIND KEY

BEAVER POND KEY

www.ingramcontent.com/pod-product-compliance
Lightning Source LLC
Chambersburg PA
CBHW051346290326
41933CB00042B/3311